Neal Mason

LOVE CAN WAIT

This edition first published in paperback by
Michael Terence Publishing in 2024
www.mtp.agency

Copyright © 2024 Neal Mason

Neal Mason has asserted the right to be identified as
the author of this work in accordance with the
Copyright, Designs and Patents Act 1988

ISBN 9781800948358

No part of this publication may be reproduced, stored
in a retrieval system, or transmitted, in any form or
by any means, electronic, mechanical, photocopying,
recording or otherwise, without the prior
permission of the publisher

Cover image
Pixabay
www.pixabay.com

Cover design
Copyright © 2024 Michael Terence Publishing

Michael Terence
Publishing

To R. H.

Contents

Motive 1
Duxford Museum, 2 a.m. 2
Bader's Bunny 4
D-Day Transporter 5
11th May 1937 6
Flight Sergeant Dennis Copping 8
Horsa 9
Arms Museum 11
Dropping In 12
G7es (T4) Falke 14
Motif 15
Escape 16
Incidental Music 17
Scharnhorst 19
A Soldier of the War 1939 - 1945 Known Unto God 21
How was your day, Ray? 22
Speer in Spandau 23
Speeding Up 25
Alterations 26
Submerged 27

Intelligence Officer	32
The Isle of Wight	34
Stringbags	35
Attitude	37
Perfidious Albion	39
Ghouls	41
Fragment	43
General Map Room, Whitehall	44
Unsinkable Sam	47
HMS Nelson	49
Whanfried, 5th April 1945	50
Upgrading Planes, 1943	52
Sword Beach	53
St. Mary's, Great Bircham	54
Acknowledgements	55
Previous Poetry Publications by Neal Mason	56

Motive

In Edward the Confessor's time,
a summer visitor, the swift, from another clime,
after flying non-stop for months,
even sleeping on the wing, settled
on Edward's coat of arms, disguised itself
as a martlet, a footless symbol
of perseverance suitable for a king.

Choosing this land for its nest,
it bred a hardy ethos that honoured the quest,
landless fourth sons seeking
fiery dragons with which to strive, struggle
enhancing the value of treasure or grail,
recognition that a sustained challenge
enables persistence to thrive.

Many years flew.
A debate, 'King and Country', voted to construe
determination another way, deciding
never to fight and die. The resolution
impressed the new German leader while,
on Oxford colleges' coats of arms,
martlets, finding their feet, cast
enquiring glances at the sky.

Duxford Museum, 2 a.m.

Brooding on their past, half-seen
shapes guard secrets, yesterday
deep in shadow. Threatening outlines
blur in memory, gunsights and barrels
aimed at targets far away, long ago.
Seized engines roar again
in cavernous silence, orders commanding
long-dead limbs, every action
imperative, static dials red-lining.

Flying jacket undone, leather helmet
in hand, a pilot stands by
his Hurricane's roundels. Linen fuselage
smelling of dope – a quick repair
after today's action – tonight his squadron
won't be scrambled, moon left in peace.
Life-expectancy rapidly decreasing,
his world seems deterministic, a machine,
every cog enmeshed. Today though, something
changed. Twenty-seven-litre Merlin engine
blazing through heaven, he caught
in his sights more than an ME 109
heading straight towards him. Closing
speed six hundred miles an hour,
machine guns hammering, the world
paused. Every event, an academic told him,
has an antecedent, free will
merely a concept thrown on a shelf
as the Hurricane's had been. His thoughts,
not being matter, broke out of cloud,
the challenging of fate at least a choice,
even if he couldn't change it. Instead

of pulling away, he would meet
the future, however short, head on.
At nearly his last moment,
the Messerschmitt disintegrated,
debris flashing past, grazing
his fuselage. When it comes to it,
he decided, determination is inbuilt,
unaffected by thinking's fresh camouflage.

The Museum's cat, a hunter-killer
obeying unwritten orders, senses
scanning the dark, effortlessly leaps
onto a wing, slides into the cockpit
and curls asleep. REM sleep, the haunt
of paradox, watches realism, a nebulous
cat-and-mouse existence among
yesterday's solid ideas.

Bader's Bunny

I live at Coltishall now, a short hop
from the open road and Douglas's MG,
display case my Colditz, a safer place to be.
But an engine-free world with sedentary habits
grows boring; I've been gawped at for years,
anecdotes breeding like rabbits,
whereas we used to rove, man and mascot,
red-lining through all the gears.

Which may explain my shade of bilious green.
Thankfully, he neglected to take me up in his plane;
rabbits aren't designed to fly in a Hurricane.
I'm all ears when it comes to a lark,
happy to break King's Regs,
but not when the humour grows dark;
you seriously think I'd like to go up
with a pilot who's lacking in legs?

If I could, I'd draw myself up to my full height
(of seven inches) Battle-of-Britain proud,
to think of his aerial courage; and time can't cloud
his escape attempts which, ears amuck,
I listened to with awe, while I,
despite my rabbit's-foot luck,
lie forgotten at home, waiting in vain
for snuggles the decades deny.

D-Day Transporter

Fixed on our grid
with nowhere to race to,
vision limited
by a bulkhead horizon,
we bank and sway
in unison, lean
for the sea bends,
vying for positions
we can't alter.

We speed ahead,
handbrakes fully applied,
steering wheels obstinate
to commands, the grey-green
camouflaged armour
like sculpted sea water,
every dial at rest,
waiting, impassive,
despite our strain.

Diesels rumble deep
below, the powers that propel us,
as though individual effort
were a spurious thing. Suspension
grumbles to itself, as if
a chained neighbour could collide,
while, outside, the threat
of more-than-shipwreck looms,
all-encompassing as the sea.

11th May 1937

'Your Majesty, it's about the guest list
for tomorrow's coronation.'
'What about it? Any changes?'
'Er, not – that is to say...'
'What on earth's the matter with you?
You can't be pissed; it's too early in the day.'
'It's the representative from the German nation.'
'Blomberg? What about him?'
'Someone's just flown in to Croydon airport
to replace him.'
'At this late stage? Someone of equal rank and station?'
'Someone who has self-selected without referring,
so I'm told, to protocol or even manners.'
'Who is it?'
'Hermann Göring.'
'What! He's just bombed half of bloody Spain!'
'And he's just arrived at Croydon unannounced,
in his bright-red, swastika-decorated plane.'
'It's not possible! What shall we do?'
'We could call Ribbentrop; tell him it risks
damaging Hitler and Germany's reputation.'
'He's suddenly fathomed the ironic? You,
of all people, know what he's like.'
'Herr Göring seems more popular
than Ribbentrop and he expressed sympathy
at the royal bereavement.'

'Being more popular than Ribbentrop
is hardly an achievement. Dammit,
I shouldn't be King anyway. It's all the fault
of my brother – and his unsuitable,
politically-suspect, twice-divorced lover.
What benefit has he ever provided
by pulling his selfish stunts?'
'Well, Your Majesty, in the past few minutes,
you haven't stammered once'

Note: Göring was dissuaded from his intentions by the German embassy and left England twelve hours after arriving.

Flight Sergeant Dennis Copping

Relocating a P-40 Kittyhawk in Egypt
before the El Alamein attack, experienced
though only twenty-four, you probably
encountered flak. Undercarriage already
damaged, miles off course, you disappeared
into the Sahara, hope your only resource.
There follows a long silence.
Regimes changed, astronauts feted,
world busy with other wars until,
in 2012, your plane was located.
Propellers bent, guns still loaded,
fuselage sandblasted, it still waited.
Parachute for shelter – shreds remain –
you huddled from daytime heat
and night's cold. No rescue came.
Without food or water, you must have decided
to walk, wandering in mind,
and still be out there somewhere,
a windswept mound, miles from anywhere,
never to be found.

Horsa

A Halifax hauled us up
like a dog on a lead, then unleashed us.
Weather uncertain, the bomber's engines
faded and we were alone, cable and thoughts
freed. Silent among the stars, we slid
through air, twenty-three soldiers,
five engineers and two pilots suddenly aware
of every creak and draught. Somewhere,
also loaded with Ox. and Bucks., two other
gliders groped their way, no power,
guns or armour, more like seeds
blown in the wind than fighting craft.
Other seeds, long ago, became the wood
for this plane, even controls carpentered,
this high in the sky normally beyond
such smooth and polished grain.
Instruments basic and few, altimeter,
compass and stopwatch told us
we were six thousand feet over Normandy,
helpless and heading for danger; things
we already knew. Below lay fields
of 'Rommel's asparagus' – posts to impede
landing – but, in a flimsy tube, it was
mines we mainly feared. At a hundred
miles an hour, we seemed merely to drift,
then sensed a dip as we angled down and,
a lunar gift, the River Orne appeared.

We didn't need wings to understand
a patch of grass, darkness and no go-round
gave us just one chance to land.
We touched down at fifteen minutes
past midnight, the sixth of June,
just seventy yards from a bridge,
our objective. We took it, spearheading
Overlord, our Horsa's passive appearance
belying it use, first in, silent,
unexpected.

Arms Museum

A collage of styles, Tudor to present,
its appearance alarms, so I reconnoitre
the outside first. A model of a soldier, gestalt
harlequin of opaque diamonds, stands guard
behind leaded glass, a challenging proto-cubist.
The Georgian window detaches him, rational
as building blocks, dimple for a heart,
while the sash window, First War, quarters
the man, a pane distorting his face. But,
at the modern wing, a sheet of armoured plate
glass, I abruptly realise he's too figurative,
not a model at all, and reflect
that, this glass broken, the complete image
will be lost.

Dropping In

People laugh. It's a fine joke.
'Have you heard the one about the gunner
who bailed out of his burning Lancaster?
Alkemade was the bloke. A Flight Sergeant,
flames kissing his arse, he launched himself
into the air more than three miles up
and landed safely. The detail that turns it
to farce, though he wasn't to blame,
is he'd left his ruddy parachute
inside the ruddy plane!'

All true. Before you could say
Nachtjagdgeschwader Zwei,
a Junkers night fighter had blown
our hopes away. On fire,
perspex knocked out, the choice was frighteningly
simple: burn to death or jump (my parachute
beyond reach, no room in the tail).
With a shout, I leapt at the night,
literally seeing stars,
the only things in sight.

I lost consciousness, the air being thin,
then felt calm sorrow at missing home,
frigid thoughts awaiting the end
and forever to begin. Then, alert,
I found myself on my back, looking still
at the stars, though through a gap in pine branches.
I was bedded in snow without footprint
or track, apparently alive.
Was this a freak accident
mere fortune contrived?

I lay there, no bones broken,
a twisted knee immobilising me,
so I blew my whistle, then smoked a Player's.
Farmers, awoken, came to investigate.
I was given medical care. Apart from splinters
of wood and perspex, and being singed at the edges,
I could hardly complain, uncomplicated
to repair. The Gestapo's view,
less sanguine than mine,
doubted my story was true.

They investigated. The Lancaster's wreck,
not far away, contained my parachute,
burned, their becoming convinced finally
saving my neck; I wasn't a spy.
They even provided proof; a certificate to show
I wasn't a dingbat who believed he could fly, nor
the Clark Kent of Bomber Command.
The truth won me acclaim,
feted me, but made me resolve
to think twice about flying again.

G7es (T4) Falke

Fired without the aid of a periscope,
the electric Falcon acoustic torpedo
flies bubble-free, listens intently.
On aquatic tiptoes, U603, later to disappear
for ever in the Atlantic, stops engines,
or the hunter might prey on its parent.
The torpedo hears

> underwater winds,
> whales making long-distance calls,
> pistol shrimps that clutch
> passing echoes of quakes
> half a world away,
> turbulent porpoises,
> sand turning in its sleep, rain
> beating the surface,
> terns diving for dinner,
> marine worms popping as they contest
> two square inches of territory.

At a steady twenty knots, it single-mindedly
seeks fresh prey, a twenty-four-foot-long
battery-powered predator. Rumbling
engines alert sensors, sensing blood,
alter course as it arcs gracefully
towards a merchantman, surprised
and surprising meal a vegetarian blowout
on grain and fresh fruit.

Motif

Love can wait.
Where conflict strives, survival
and mere sex predominate Yet Tommy
sacrificed himself, risking his life
for his mate. It had little to do
with agape, nor considered action
after debate; something unthinking
drove him, commitment to a cause
he didn't realise he valued so much.
Nor was it really hate, the enemy
also adhering to a sense of duty
and loyalty to the state. There was fear
of shame, he knew; the terror of letting
oneself down always great, but something
inside knew what to do, conviction
innate. The drive to survive stays strong,
but not absolute, societies resorting,
in desperate times, to the recurrent trait.
Love can wait.

Escape

Just a brush,
wood and bristles, a Red Cross afterthought
so a prisoner of war might sweep away fluff
or distractions. Or keep no-longer-Brylcreemed
hair flat, tidy thoughts. Perhaps shoes need cleaning
for the parade ground of the past,
fiancé and family home receding, childhood
a toy left out in the rain.
Just a brush, yet
this one comes apart, reveals inside
a silken map. Scrubbed clean, fresh hope
wishes away patrolled roads, sentry posts
and wire in freedom's path. Dejection lifts
like grime as plans are refreshed, polished
in a secret landscape to wander
during quiet moments. He loses himself
among pine, birch, copper beech, glimpses
deer, quail, pheasant; even a bristled
wild boar among migrating waders.
He dusts off plans with the Escape Committee
less urgently as time passes, sidetracked
along scenic routes hidden in folds. Years
escape in his absence, camp incidental,
mind free in the private landscape
he feels at home in, sent in a parcel.
Just a brush.

Incidental Music

The LSO, Queen's Hall, August 1940

Proms popular, full Hall
defying the Blitz, the audience, uplifted
by music, would now like to leave; but Fritz
disturbs the famed acoustic with his own.
There's no 'all clear'. Orchestra and public
stay all night, request songs they've known
since young and hold dear,
the confronting of providence a leitmotif
that will not consent to submit. The Hall
will be silent and empty by the time it's hit.

The Berlin Philharmonic, April 1945

Concert hall intense, lit only
by music stands, multiple shells
provide a drum roll. Players' hands,
now steady, raise instruments and bows,
a final act of resistance, the beginning of the end
of 'Götterdämmerung', for, as everyone knows,
music holds life at a distance
for a while. Speer has provided transport,
but the orchestra has decided to stay; fatalism
will have it so. There's no other way.

Beethoven's violin concerto follows.
Anguished, dejected, gripping fate
by the throat, he fought deafness, suicide rejected.
The Third Reich, reaping calamity,
chaos and destruction in charge, must soon succumb
to a vengeful red mist, the triumph of insanity.

Bruckner looms large,
his Fourth Symphony's cathedral of sound
the only building that will stand; art,
a survivor, will scratch a living in this land.

The strains approach the end and it's time
for leave-taking and tears. At the exit,
Hitler Youth, mature though young in years,
proffer baskets of cyanide pills.
Dreading Berlin's fate, thousands will die
by their own hand; in London, suicide kills
fewer than the peacetime rate.
Such trumpets and drums sound muffled now,
coda fading away, though never
quite gone, still echoing today.

Scharnhorst

Boxing Day, nineteen forty-three.
A few decorations, the odd beer barrel,
even a Christmas tree. A constant choir,
ululating wind singing its own carol,
blizzards north of Norway seldom tire,
seas heavy and black, sailors longing
for home and a sea-coal fire.
Konteradmiral Bey considers turning back,
but is ordered on, a convoy reported, so
battleship Scharnhorst follows her destroyers,
gale-blown outlines distorted. Her mere
existence exerts a grip on Admiralty minds;
she's sunk many an Allied ship, not least
the aircraft carrier Glorious, Scharnhorst
perversely buoyed by heavy armour plate,
nine eleven-inch guns and the expectation
of emerging victorious. Gradually,
she loses touch with her destroyers.
Bey suspects enemy forces close, but not
that they lie in wait, that a trap has been set
using the convoy as bait. He plots positions,
sets a course for Bear Island, sends a message
of progress, unaware the British can read
Enigma's transmissions. Shielded by storms,
he's turned off his radar in case it's detected
but, nearby, HMS Belfast and Force One,
similarly storm-protected, haven't. Belfast
informs Force Two that Scharnhorst's destroyers
have turned back, supplies co-ordinates
directors require, then, with Norfolk and Sheffield
at twelve thousand yards, opens fire.

Unexpected, eight-inch shells, imprecise
though radar-directed, sting Scharnhorst,
who replies with her own salvos, although
hit twice. The first makes little impact,
failing to explode; the second destroys
antennae, only aft radar left intact.
On Norfolk, a turret burns, superstructure
awry. Scharnhorst, breaking off, turns,
outruns pursuers to seek the elusive convoy
for another try. What she finds
is Force Two. Difficult to escape, the larger fleet
includes the battleship Duke of York. Star shells
illuminate the sea, a witch's brew,
the battle of the North Cape. York's fourteen-inch
shells set Scharnhorst's forward turret
on fire, disable ventilation to the middle turret,
noxious fumes forcing gunners to retire.
Another shell disrupts the boiler room,
reducing her speed. York too has damage,
though less severe, fires fifty-two salvos
with thirteen hits, would continue,
but there's no need. Bey and Scharnhorst know
the end is near. Force Two's destroyers
launch torpedoes. Scharnhorst shudders, lists
to starboard, resisting still. Commitment
and duty comply with the Captain's will, prevail
over staying alive. Scharnhorst sinks
at nineteen-fifteen that Boxing Day.
Of a nearly two thousand crew,
thirty-six survive.

A Soldier of the War
1939 - 1945
Known Unto God

Suda Bay reflects, calm now.
The decades have passed quietly,
much of Crete the wonder it was.
Teenagers, younger than you, play
with water pistols, tomorrow
unhurried, slow to come.

Holidaymakers invade, occupy
the north coast, Greece importing
a kind of culture washed away
with the tide. But here I remember
an old woman walking slowly,
a sense of loss drifting
among graves.

Wondering, years of looking
over her shoulder, a sudden
mistaken voice. One day
she didn't come back, see
what look like azaleas –
what's in a name? – prolific
blue ending to this June day.

Above the heat, myths and everyday
dust, Mount Ida, headstone
for Minos, glints evening
sunshine on snow. An era
passed like a day, ruins
in shadows, lost names

known unto God.

How was your day, Ray?

15th September 1940

Located three Dornier bombers over Surrey.
Latched onto one, but suddenly a slurry
of something black hit my screen – oil
from a flamethrower in the Dornier's tail;
something I'd never seen. The oil didn't light,
luckily, but totally obscured all sight
until my Hurricane was cleaned by the stream
of air from the prop. Above me flew the green,
looming shape, but ahead, at a lower height,
was another, and he was in my sight. I fired.
A white shape emerged; a man bailing out.
My plane lurched. With an involuntary shout,
I looked around and saw a strange thing;
a parachute, with man attached, adorned my starboard wing.
I weaved, managed to shake him free
and saw the third Dornier ahead of me.
Without considering my aircraft's condition,
I aimed – but was out of ammunition.
We were over London, so I made a decision;
I could end his sortie with a minor collision,
my intention being to clip his tail fin.
I overdid it. His tail fell off, he went into a spin.
My plane too had had enough for one day,
wouldn't respond, so we went our separate ways,
though not before it gave me a clout
as I struggled with the canopy and bailed out.
I watched, detached, feeling neither pride nor malice
as the Dornier crashed near Buckingham Palace,
its bombs falling out on the way down.
My own descent, boots missing, on London town
ended on a roof, from which I slid, cussing,
landing ignominiously in a dustbin.

Ray Holmes 1914 - 2005

Speer in Spandau

If I construct
columns, like so, beanpoles
for the imagination …
or guide the attention
to a triumphal arch
of three roses ….
or, perhaps, plant daffodils
like searchlights, focal point
a narcissus – but that
would be out of proportion.

I design with little space,
no lebensraum. Armed
with spade and hoe, I could annex
the path, a march of five paces,
reorganise the grass,
divide it with a hedge
like a wall …

Flowers or food?
I used to be so good
at planning, but now
I'm an architect without
materials. What I could do with
a suburban garden.

In the greenhouse
of my mind, I tend
even weeds, select between
something and nothing. I grow,
year after year, a more
balanced view, find even
irregularities natural.
And only a lifetime ago
this was dust, field grey.

Each bloom, each tuber and fruit
a monument, I learn
about vegetation. A leaf
seems massive now, a miracle
of construction, and though
I control resources, guide
nature's little war, I envy
her power, her energy,
her freedom.

Speeding Up

When Hitler looked east, blinkered
cavalry still cantered in defenders' forces
and the High Command's mind, until, suddenly,
galloping headlong, events left old-fashioned
horsepower behind. And the Swordfish,
open bi-plane, continued flying when the Meteor,
the Allies first jet, took off. War concentrates
the mind. So slow, German gunners miscalculated
range, the Swordfish was overtaken by a jet
five times as fast; equally strange, the British
feared it falling into enemy hands, its secrets
preventing use in foreign lands. Little did they know.
The Messerschmitt 262, with an engine
different in design, constructed in difficult
conditions, made the Meteor look slow.
Like a racehorse, it couldn't wait,
temperamental engine's life a mere
twenty-five hours; for a day anyway
it left the rest at the starting gate,
outpacing rivals produced by the Allies.
Yet, despite its speed, it arrived
too late.

From bi-planes to jets, a hurried
few years, radar and rocket development
striding on, as did production
of the atom bomb. All had peacetime
benefits unimagined before, as though
the imagination were trained
by unimaginable war.

Alterations

I didn't so much jump as tumble
out of my Spitfire's cockpit. Cannon shells
struck the Merlin engine, magic roar
becoming a grumble, fury unspoken,
then stopped, Messrs Rolls and Royce
powerless, the spell broken.

Apart from the fear of being shot
(a few pilots scorned the concept of chivalry)
it was pleasant enough parachuting down.
I never forgot, despite my burns,
I owed my life, not only to planners,
but a host of industrious worms.

Landing in Kent, I gathered my bundle,
contacted the police and was taken back to base.
I made my report, still high on adrenalin,
words a jumble, and later I slept,
relieved of my scorched and tatty clothes,
but the silken parachute I kept.

Alice and I were engaged for a year,
but not any more. Today, a white wedding
alters our status, though money's still tight,
everything dear. Most things on ration,
we make do and mend, but her silk dress
looks splendid, the height of fashion!

Submerged

The coffin belly flops, alarmed
sea leaping aside, then flooding back
like recurring memories
committed to the deep.

On its long descent, falling
from sunlight compressed into essence,
it slews by sleek shapes, disturbs
sea-bed sand before settling
to cold contemplation.

Coffined in metal, but costumed
like his living world of blue
and gold, the Admiral rests below
Atlantic storms he fought
all his life. Long ago begins
to seep back, raw as wartime,
chill orders releasing death
in depth-charge patterns.

Time and chance, navigating
again, guided his coffin
like a submarine. Long-settled
on the sea bed, not a cable's length
from its killer, a holed U42,
its Captain and its crew.

Deeper than sleep, an outline
in green, it meditates
on old missions. Earphones listen
for echoes of messages,
torpedoes ready in forward tubes,
dials still registering
depth, range, attitude.

The coffin waits
like a ship on silent running.

After decades of no sound
but the sliding tide, asdic
wakes the deep. It floods
sea with fear again, a living
pulse to haunt submariners'
ghosts; it prods and probes
diesel room and galley, bridge
and water-filled buoyancy tanks,
then moves on to search
adjacent sea. Black water shrouding
U42 stirs. Hydroplanes, rusty,
alter position like bodies
in sleep. Twin screws begin
to turn. Silt and years
falling away, long-entombed
bubbles breaking for the surface,
the submarine lifts; its shape
blurs, eases free, glides
silently over the coffin.

Gliding too, the funeral vessel
curves to port, nuclear-age
electronics silent, screens blank
as cloudy water. Far out to sea
a herring gull swoops,
sensing prey.

Surreptitious fish
slip past the coffin, nudge detritus,
fragments of sinking life. A crab
claws from under seaweed, fingers
the compartment's bulkhead.

On the ship, a lookout shouts,
urgent voice metallic
through earphones. Electronics
question an empty sea,
the sighting of what cannot be
a periscope. Eyes probe and scan,
dip into waves, then find
two parallel lines
becoming a vee. Speeding across years,
compressed yesterdays burst free,
angry bubbles propelling
hundreds of pounds of TNT.

The ship swerves, skids
on water, computers and crew
firing orders. A double explosion
knocks it sideways,
tilts it starboard. Ripped metal
swallows sea, automatic maydays
shouting at the sky. Survivors
bob on lifeboats, glimpse briefly
a conning tower breaking surface,
the periscope's dead eye
watching, then sinking from sight.

Encased in cold water,
the Admiral waits,
metallic gaze fixed.

U42 slides back, backtracks, black
form intent, new course plotted
years ago. Far above, old clouds gather,
re-form like a scattered convoy.
Phosphorescent wakes begin to glow
again, shipless, mist gradually
congealing, manufacturing, one by one,
grey hulls, grey faces. A destroyer,
class B, fits its wake, a determined line
homing in, targeting
transformed waves. The Admiral-to-be,
dressed in blue and gold, leans
on the ship's rail, eyes focussed
far below the surface. Asdic
reports contact. Gaze fixed,
he gives the order.

Sealed off by the sea's skin,
an underworld listens. Motion
slows, sound trickling down
as canisters splash playfully,
tumble, eddy, buffet
evasive fish.

Water erupts. Sea anemones
explode, orange flames flowering
far above, currents barged aside
as fringed tubes spout
at the sun. U42 lurches,
superstructure cracked, pressure hull
burst with eardrums. Stern down,
aerated water lowering it
reverently, it settles
back to its resting place.

Seawater clears, bubbles and detritus
going separate ways, a wash and sift
of revolving years. The periscope watches
the coffin, underwater seascape
quiescent, pressured into peace.
Water-filled, the Admiral's eye sockets
stare upwards, see himself
looking down, a figure leaning
on a ship's rail, eyes observing
oil, flotsam and jetsam and the lagan
at the bottom of his mind.

Intelligence Officer

'Armchair pilot' they call me, as though
I flicked through Bomber Command casualties
unaffected. My seemingly suspect operations
sometimes rely on rumours and half-truths
whose reasons lie undetected. Emotions motivate,
cold calculation saves lives; for me,
it's not about being 'a jolly good chap'
but my results being respected.

At de-briefings, bomber crews
reported explosions on nightly raids
and rationalised. Did the Germans have shells
called 'scarecrows', harmless but realistic
morale-shakers, devised, it was said,
to alarm? Hardly likely. But flak or a faulty timer
seemed worse, so I encouraged the rumour,
even truth nationalised.

Not surprisingly, crew casualties
and strain gave rise to superstitions,
as in sport, but with deadlier results.
They thought they'd learned the 'Identification, Friend
or Foe' transmitter could distort, electronically,
searchlight controls. It couldn't – might even be
a risk – yet qualified pilots left it on,
preferring what hope taught.

Lancasters, vulnerable to night fighters,
found they were safer at a hundred feet,
belly protected. But, cavity magnetron
invented, we had to explain how aircrews' vision
was suddenly sharper than expected. I photographed
pilots munching carrots, let it be known that eyes,
not radar, were their secret weapon. Even
today this fantasy's accepted.

The Isle of Wight

Groping in the dark, radar screens
detect nothing, Channel empty of threats,
yet unexploded rumours persist, hard
to track, that German commandos – Brandenburgers –
made a night attack in August, forty-three.
Chain Home Radar their objective, they arrived
from the sea in dinghies launched from a U-boat –
but, officially, that cannot be. German records too,
after passing through Allied hands, omit
to mention any such raid, though listing
activities in other lands. Gossip in Ventnor
suggests gunfire and flames, sea alight with oil,
burnt soldiers' bodies covertly collected,
no regiments or names. An Air Raid Warden's
diary refers to the event, but locals, interviewed
by anonymous officials, decided
they'd been misled, signing the Official Secrets Act,
it's said. Of great interest to the Germans,
radar warned of attacks, but bombing did little
to the pylons; of more interest were the operators'
shacks. Aerials were easier to restore
than equipment and personnel. Within hours
of it not happening, Junkers bombed the town,
the coast as well, while a lone Messerschmitt
took photos before being shot down.
But official records say nothing, historians'
pages blank, and this piece won't be written,
the whispers merely a prank. Secretly
invading the coast, hints and memories persist,
though radar sweeps detect merely
calm seas and the ghost of a mist.

Stringbags

Lieutenant Commander Esmonde
read the order, blanched, then prepared to do
what was expected. He knew very well
what it meant. His six Swordfish, better known
as 'Stringbags', had recently proved effective,
despite being out-dated bi-planes, open-cockpit and,
to enemy fighters, heaven-sent. Although slow,
Stringbags torpedoed the Italian Navy,
the Bismarck too – Esmonde had been there –
but to take on the Scharnhorst, Prinz Eugen,
Geneisenau and Luftwaffe cover seemed an act
of despair. The Great British top brass,
taking incompetence to a new height,
had elevated the Great British balls up
to a level only perfection could surpass.
Enigma warned of a planned Channel run,
as did French agents, captured Kriegsmarine
charts and the flagrant clue that minesweeping
had begun. Aerial reconnaissance reported
destroyers gathering at Brest, submarine
observation concurring, Admiral Otto Ciliax
taking command at Hitler's behest. To cap it all,
the weather was poor, radar in the Channel
jammed, all this and more lost on Whitehall.
For twelve hours the German squadron's
progress went undetected; only at Dover
Straits did bombers, fighters and batteries on shore
attempt to close the stable door, planes and MTBs
late and misdirected. As Esmonde and his six
Stringbags finalised approach, their fighter cover
scattered, gunfire spraying from ships,
Messerschmitts and Focke-Wulfs. The bi-planes
manoeuvred deftly, but it hardly mattered.

Esmonde was intercepted long before
his torpedo could be released, the other five
downed or blown to bits. When the attack ceased,
it was clear they, and all the bombers, batteries
and surface craft, had scored no hits.

Although hampered by mines in the North Sea,
the Kriegsmarine achieved tactical success,
humiliated the Royal Navy and delighted
the German press. Ships reached home ports
or a Norwegian fjord but, thanks to Hitler,
the grander strategy was flawed. The relocation
had intended to resist, it was later revealed,
a British invasion of Norway, but no such plan
was ever shown to exist. In time, Royal Naval
supremacy restored, the German ships were sunk
or disabled. Esmonde and his Stringbags, feted
and fabled, duty selflessly faced, became both heroes
and victims of senseless waste.

Attitude

A bit too old for active service, Smith
awaits his air-raid-warden's shift, reads,
puzzled, 'British Empiricists', a book
found lying around – someone's unwanted gift,
or fallout from the bombed library, a tatty
remnant, though perfect bound.

He fingers pages – they smell of smoke – ears
alert for the incoming hum of a raid. A sip
of tea makes reading more palatable, but attention,
eyeing the scene, practical, begins to fade.
Empiricism makes sense, but a siren
begins its distracting keen.

A bit too old for active service, Schmidt
begins his day in the control tower. Aircraft
aren't expected yet, so he studies
'German Idealists' – after all, knowledge is power.
It seems the world's an idea, a vision
misunderstood by realists.

Via National Socialism, he touches on Kant,
Fichte and Hegel, sensing affinity. He imagines
objectives, utopian, worthy of commitment,
then ponders Marx. Materialist sublimity?
How have eastern enemies taken
this German to their hearts?

When the shrapnel starts flying,
it doesn't remain in the head,
except literally. In every sense,
Smith and Schmidt experience the world,
stains testifying where they bled.
Philosophy's biased affinities
hold little interest for the dead

Perfidious Albion

'You can't deny it! Naval Intelligence
took photographs; a division of tanks
in South-West England.'
'Yes Kommodore, but – '
'You realise the risk my sailors took? –
not that I expect much thanks,
you being a pen-pushing landlubber.'
'True, I admit. But it's also true
the tanks were made of rubber.'

'You said that about the armour
in Scotland. The whole of Britain is rubberised?
It's your head that's going soft!
First, you say they constructed
wooden artillery – ' 'Which we bombed
with wooden bombs.' 'Then they disguised
factories as farms, spread false accounts,
it seems, about Southampton's damage
and attacked us with bombs that bounce!

'And why didn't they deploy their 5th
Airborne Division in Italy? We waited.'
'I'm afraid it didn't exist'
'Wonderful. It wasn't just
their pretend boats, transport and soft
armour; their numbers too were inflated!
They dropped dummy parachutists behind our lines,
employed actors to ape commanders
and planted misleading road signs!

'The English were always odd, but are now
barking, as though a memory of Dali,
persistent, had grown in their brains
and rendered their world surreal;
a distorted view's mutated
to an out-of-control Svengali.
They laid, in North Africa, a pipeline for water,
only for show, their army elsewhere.
We were led like lambs to the slaughter.

'They employed a magician – I'm serious –
to make the Suez disappear,
carefully-positioned searchlights
and revolving mirrors for props,
while, up their sleeves, the Tommies
secreted double agents here;
troops and face were only part of our losses.
To cap it all, we rewarded their agents
with two Iron Crosses!'

Ghouls

Rime on charred beams.
Shafts of sunrise
prop walls, mist rising
like smoke. a blue roof
instead of slate grey.
Looters, faces wrapped
against the chill,
have already been.
Turneresque dawn
just a glare, onlookers
shade eyes, wind scarves
for warmth. They point
icy fingers, words
a heavy vapour,
cheeks glowing
bright as sunshine
in a dead grate. Exposed
bedroom an orgy
of frozen panic,
gazes singe sheets, stain
clothes, sympathy tinged
by a sort of lust.

Firemen and wardens did what they could,
digging up the night,
wrapping remains, isolating
incendiaries. They rake up
no excuses, prurience
ranked with the enemy, fan
no embers of mitigation.

A chimney pot leans,
cold, as though no smoke
meant no fire. Miles high,
puffs of cloud edge away,
buff heaven, spread
messages like smoke signals,
the gossip of the sky.

Fragment

A fourteen-year-old boy, Eric Horne
has heard of V2 rockets, Germany's new
wonder-weapon. He shrugs, hands in pockets,
and wanders home, thoughts moving on.
He's in the living-room when a blast,
louder than a normal bomb, showers him
with wood and glass. The V2 landed streets away,
killing fourteen people and, to him, Lewisham
changed profoundly that day. He receives
medical aid, relieved to find no serious
harm, unaware one small consequence
has been delayed.

A ninety-two-year-old man, Eric Horne
rubbed his face. He'd long ago emigrated
to Australia, become a policeman, settling
with a new family in a new place.
Recalling, he rubbed his face again.
Something irritated under the skin.
Manipulating tweezers, ignoring the slight
pain, he extracted a small piece of metal
from above his chin. An acquaintance
examined it, a small aluminium sliver, and saw,
to his surprise, lettering, a font common
in Germany during the War. The fragment
of the past, carried seventy-seven years,
transported him back to another world,
its hopes and fears, enormity reduced
to this tiny trace, now preserved in a museum's
glass-covered display case

General Map Room, Whitehall

Pinholes perforate the sea, tiny
explosions on paper. Convoys dot
their way over water, invisible
U-boats under the table, worming up
through wood. The sea bed
far below is carpeted
with litter, lost fountain pen
a spent torpedo. God,
rings on his cuffs, moves
the sun north, a sixty watt glare
at Archangel, cups coffee
in both hands, tired eyes
quartering the freezing sea.

Shivering in the dog watch,
A.B. Clark grips his mug
for warmth, scans grey waves,
the surface of the sea
like screwed up paper. Hope
detects the escort come to meet them,
soon fades into mist and spray. Lamed
by yesterday's wolf pack, radio gone,
they straggle behind convoy PQ17,
only foul weather and heavy seas
keeping the freighter and A.B. Clark
afloat. If there's a God watching above
squalls of sleet, successive gales,
let Him not overlook
this speck on the ocean
loaded with lorries and grief.
Later, colder, his prayers swearwords,
his fears prayers, an explosion
perforates the sea.

The ringed cuff hesitates,
inches the pin eastwards
across miles of water, PQ17
breasting creases. Off the map,
pins litter a shelf, a tangle of metal.
A sigh of cigar smoke
spreads from the White Sea, Clark
grateful for mist, answer to a prayer
that hides the listing freighter
from U-boats and planes. At this latitude,
in this season, night never comes,
the sun's glare a lamp
always on, another target
for Clark's curses. The Admiralty
had ordered their escort to leave,
the convoy to scatter
and dissolve in mist. Suddenly,
strained eyes half-detecting
shadows in the east, his hope
solidifies into shapes, an escort
and safety. Brain freezing, hands
thinking for themselves, he anticipates
the bridge, operates his Aldis,
an urgent message
of position, damage, welcome.

The message clutched in the hand
with ringed cuffs, body slumped
in a chair, comes from Norway.
The *Tirpitz*, with a battle group,
has left port to attack PQ17, but then
tuned back. The convoy's escorts departed
to confront the *Tirpitz*, scattered
convoy unprotected. No wake of dots
betraying progress, ghost ships roam
a ghost ocean. A U-boat plans
a new course until, like an answer
to a prayer, an Aldis flickers
through fog. Guttural orders alert
senses, make out a listing freighter,
a sitting target pinpointed
by an intermittent lamp, a dot
with an urgent message
of position, damage, welcome.

Unsinkable Sam

Not my real name, of course. I'm Oscar
and you're pleased to meet me. Distinguished,
I swopped sides during the War, allowing no shell,
bomb or torpedo to defeat me.

I served first on the battleship Bismarck, which I thought
a safe posting. I don't make mistakes,
but, water lapping round my ears, I almost
considered forsaking boasting.

Rescued and treated by His Majesty's Ship Cossack,
one of the enemy, I quickly decided (never
being good at the Hitler salute) to recognise
the Royal Navy's hegemony.

Language not being a problem, I began my duties
chasing vermin. I'd hardly settled in
when there was a loud bang, a general alarm, soon
followed by the smell of burning.

Cossack, torpedoed, listed and sank. Undignified,
covered in oil, I lolloped into a lifeboat,
reached Gibraltar and received my next assignment; the unsinkable Ark Royal.

You guessed it. She was torpedoed soon after.
If I were a cod, I'd surely spend less time
in water and, short of lives, I resented being called
an old sea dog.

Enough is enough. I opted for shore duties, never more to roam. Still sharp and an excellent mouse-catcher, I spent the rest of my life in England in a retired sailors' home.

Note: Oscar graciously consented to sit for his portrait, which he expects you to go and see at the National Maritime Museum in Greenwich.

HMS Nelson

Three torpedoes speed towards the battleship
with eight hundred yards to live, the distance
between U56 and detonation. The fist torpedo hits
without exploding. So does the second.
But the third
misses entirely, setting off
rumours of invincibility, at least
for the duration. The bridge
saw death appear with no train of bubbles,
torpedoes breaking on impact, fate
toying with the moment and the lives
of the crew: will I? won't I? expected
or out of the deep blue?
From U56, a burst of invective
aimed at German efficiency, the T2 torpedo,
its contact detonator infuriatingly
ineffective.

Bombed, shelled and mined, HMS Nelson
serves throughout the War, escorting
Atlantic convoys, helping invade Algeria,
Italy and Normandy, surviving them all
and more. From Death, a burst of invective
aimed at industrious shipyards
and stubborn sailors, grinning luck
for an ensign. HMS Nelson
retires peacefully
to be scrapped in nineteen forty-nine.

Whanfried, 5th April 1945

Portraits line the walls:
Beethoven, Goethe and other
members of my family. Also
more distant relations
like my parents.

The bombs falling now,
the devastation they say
I helped orchestrate, destroys
the living room, furniture,
books and scores. But
not the music. A temporary
Götterdämmerung.

The gods will survive.
Had Leningrad fallen,
would the Seventh perish?
Like mine, his music
goes to war, called up
with Glinka, Tchaikovsky
and other members of our family.

Being immortal,
why should we fight?
Library and drawing room
restored, what difference to us
whether it's Marx or Nietzsche's
incendiary work replaced?

Hitler, Stalin
or other members of their family
line us up against their walls.
But creation, not destruction,
our motif, the music
is not the book, nor the Battle
Symphony war.

Guilty of prejudice,
of martial music, of conquering
leaders, we transgress,
but show me the artist
with no darkness and I'll show you
why he died unremembered.

Upgrading Planes, 1943

Good morning, Group Captain. I'm phoning
to inform you about Churchill's new plane,
despite the secrecy it's wrapped in.
It's an Avro 685 York – a bloated Lancaster
by another name – so a few specifications
will suffice. To fool the Huns, we've fitted
every modern device, except guns. They'd never
expect that. There's a heated toilet seat,
ash trays for his cigar, magazine racks
and, of course, a bar. We discarded unnecessary
extras, like a pressurised cabin; by keeping low,
you can fly foxier – besides, war's funnier
when you're affected by hypoxia (I've been reading
Byron, you know). There's a radio connection
to the crew – good luck with that; with two
Merlin engines in each ear, words will necessarily
be few. It has a long range and good speed,
but a warning; don't let the Old Boy
pilot the thing. Clemmie insists it's streng verboten.
If he pulls such a stunt, she might look
inoffensive, but will out-glare one-eyed Wotan
and open her own second front. By the way,
the plane's been paganly Christened 'Ascalon'
after St. George's lance; it seems, this time,
the dragon's to be given a better chance.

Sword Beach

Sunbathing bodies strewn on sand, castles
abandoned, serried waves advance
up the beach. Footprints erased, June asserts
this is a wish-you-were-here
postcard of a place, the only danger
ice-cream-stealing gulls.
Boats aim prows landwards,
trippers observing a ball's tiny
explosions of sand, boys' shrieks and screams
chasing up dunes. Overhead,
the glint of an airliner
evading clouds' camouflage, radar
alert for a sudden storm. A gust
from the sea sweeps towards
the coast road, past litter bins
holding yesterday's papers, houses,
blinds drawn as though they've seen
too much, then safely over
a pedestrian crossing to the vast
expanse of Normandy which beckons
the visitor on.

St. Mary's, Great Bircham

Outnumbered now, eleven airmen
of the Luftwaffe, gravestones rigidly in line,
confront serried enemies – not enemies,
but opponents, said one, dead nonetheless.
War calls up lies, seldom euphemisms,
men not passing away, no longer with us,
but killed. Each headstone, regardless
of umlauts, declensions, pronunciation,
speaks a sermon, visitor comprehending
far more than breeze and bird calls.
Like Hardrada, they invaded the land,
securing one tiny bit of it, never
to go home, but locals care for their graves
no less than the others. Norfolk accents
bend carved names, dates caring
not a jot for language. Helmut Seidel,
shot down by Guy Gibson's Beaufighter,
washed up on shore three months later,
already a memory. Others were never found.
At least his name survives, like one
listed in the Iliad, where and how he fell,
little else. At the time, it was only life;
looked back on, if he could look back,
it was all, though never valued at its
full rate.

Acknowledgements

'Arms Museum' and 'D-Day Transporter' were first published in slightly altered versions by Peterloo Poets.

'Submerged', 'Speer in Spandau', 'General Map Room, Whitehall' and 'Whanfried, 5th April 1945' were first published by the University of Salzburg Press.

'Ghouls' was published in an earlier version by Smiths Knoll.

'Speeding Up' first appeared on the soundwork-uk.co.uk website.

'Upgrading Planes, 1943' was shortlisted in The Letter Review poetry competition.

'Flight Sergeant Dennis Copping' was longlisted in the Butcher's Dog magazine competition.

'Unsinkable Sam' was Highly Commended in the Ver Poets' competition and published in their anthology.

Previous Poetry Publications by Neal Mason

Poetry Preview 2
(Peterloo Poets 1990)

Excavations
(Peterloo Poets 1991)

Leading the Guidebook Astray
(University of Salzburg Press 1995)

The Past is a Dangerous Driver
(Holland Park Press 2022)

*Available worldwide from Amazon
and all good bookstores*

www.mtp.agency

www.facebook.com/mtp.agency

@mtp_agency

www.ingramcontent.com/pod-product-compliance
Lightning Source LLC
LaVergne TN
LVHW051219070526
838200LV00064B/4974